TSUNAMI

THE TRUE STORY OF AN
APRIL FOOLS' DAY DISASTER

GAIL LANGER KARWOSKI
ILLUSTRATED BY JOHN MACDONALD

DARBY
CREEK
PUBLISHING

To my writers' group: Susan Vizurraga, Bettye Stroud, Donny Seagraves, Muriel Pritchett, Lori Hammer, Lola Finn, Jackie Elsner, and Cindy Crain—who have survived (and improved) many of my manuscripts

With special thanks to:

- *Dr. Walter C. Dudley, Director of Kalakaua Marine Education Center and Professor of Oceanography, University of Hawaii at Hilo*

- *Dr. Gilles Allard, Emeritus Professor of Geology, University of Georgia*

- *Dr. Lori Dengler, Professor and Chair, Department of Geology, Humboldt State University*

- *my husband and first reader, Dr. Chester Karwoski, Emeritus Professor of Psychology, University of Georgia*

- *Kawaihona Laeha Poy of Laupahoehoe, Hawaii, for sharing her memories*

- *The Pacific Tsunami Museum, Hilo, Hawaii*

Cataloging-in-Publication

Karwoski, Gail, 1949-
Tsunami: the true story of an April Fools' Day disaster/ by Gail Langer Karwoski; [illustrations by John MacDonald].
      p. ; cm.
ISBN-13: 978-1-58196-044-0
ISBN-10: 1-58196-044-1
Summary: April Fools' Day, 1946: a sunny Hawaiian school day that started out as any other—until the ocean began to pull back, exposing the seafloor. Suddenly, someone looked up: Now a wall of water was racing toward them. This was no April Fools' joke—it was a deadly tsunami. Learn about this and other tsunamis from history.
1. Tsunamis—Juvenile literature. 2. Hawaii—History—Juvenile literature. [1. Tsunamis. 2. Hawaii—History.] I. Title. II. Author. III. Cover title: Tsunami : the true story of an April Fools' Day disaster. IV. Ill.
GC221.5 .K37 2006
363.34/9 dc22
OCLC: 63183683

Published by DARBY CREEK PUBLISHING
7858 Industrial Parkway
Plain City, OH 43064
www.darbycreekpublishing.com

Printed in Italy

1 2 3 4 5 6 7 8 9

CONTENTS

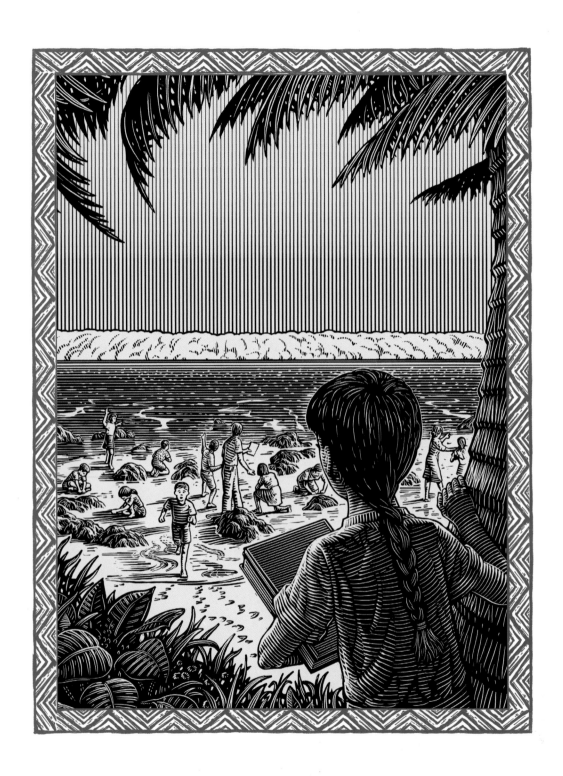

CHAPTER ONE

April Fools' Day

The school bus wound along the narrow road as the morning sun played peek-a-boo behind gray clouds. Inside the bus, an older boy swiveled to face two small girls sitting behind him. He began telling them a wild story. With a serious look, he assured them that every word he spoke was true. The dark eyes of his small listeners grew wider. Other children fell silent as they strained to hear the storyteller's words. Knowing his audience was hooked, the storyteller raised his voice and lavished his tale with ever more astounding details.

At last, the slim boy sitting beside the storyteller interrupted. "April Fools' Day!" he shouted. All the older children burst out laughing, and the small listeners blushed as they lowered their eyes.

Barely 7:00 AM on that Monday in 1946, and the day seemed to be off to a great start. The bus pulled up in front of the school. As the children spilled out, they waved at classmates walking down the slope toward the building. Everyone expected this day to be filled with silly pranks and jokes. And better yet, only one more week of classes before spring recess!

How could the children know that they would remember this April Fools' Day for its horror, not for its laughter? The Pacific Ocean was about to deliver its terrible punch line.

THE SCHOOL ON A "LEAF OF LAVA"

Laupahoehoe is a small community on the eastern side of the island of Hawaii, the southernmost island in the chain that is also called Hawaii. Nicknamed the "Big Island," Hawaii is larger than all the other islands combined. Laupahoehoe is about twenty miles north of Hilo, the largest city on the Big Island.

In 1946, Laupahoehoe School was on the point of a little peninsula of smooth lava that juts into the Pacific Ocean. In the Hawaiian language, "laupahoehoe" means "leaf of lava," which describes the peninsula's appearance. The school sat in the center of this leaf of lava. In the middle of the U-shaped school building grew a large banyan tree. Between the school and the shore was a ball field and bleachers. At the edge of the field, seven small teachers' cottages stood on stilts above the rocks at the edge of the water.

About five hundred children in grades kindergarten through twelve attended Laupahoehoe School. The classes were full of friends and neighbors. An eighth grader at the school in 1946, Frank DeCaires later recalled, "When we used to come to school, we used to know everybody."

From her classroom, first-year teacher Marsue McGinnis looked through a

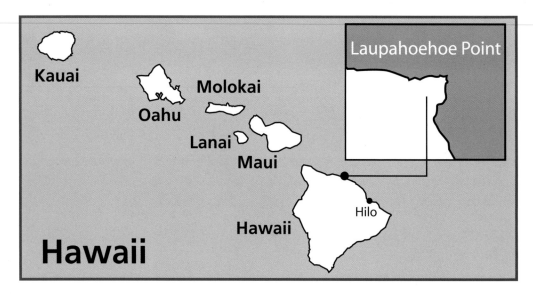

floor-to-ceiling glass window at a red hibiscus hedge. Beyond the hedge was a peaceful cemetery where a white horse was tied. The horse nibbled the greenery growing around the old gravestones.

Many times after a rain, Marsue watched waterfalls cascading off the cliffs behind the little peninsula. Her barefoot students often brought her presents of orchids and fruit, and they told her about the whales and sea turtles they had spotted in the ocean during their walks to school.

Beautiful Laupahoehoe before the 1946 tsunami

Marsue lived with three other young women teachers in one of the cottages that she described as a "stone's throw" from the sea. From her cottage or from her classroom, she said she could gaze at "the blue, blue ocean." Sometimes she swam in those aquamarine waters after school. Neighbors shared their catch of fresh fish with the young teachers. Marsue's students loved to tell her their family stories about boating in those waters.

Marsue McGinnis was twenty-one years old, and she had just graduated from a university in Ohio. As she gazed at her surroundings from her classroom and cottage, she smiled with the thought that she'd landed her first teaching job in paradise.

Vanishing Ocean

As soon as the sun came up that Monday morning, people began to notice that the ocean had an unusual appearance. It seemed to be drawing back from shore—like when water drains from a bathtub.

On the bus, some children remarked on the strange sight. Three brothers from the Fujimoto family were on board. The middle brother, a teenager named Bunji, said that kids in the front of the bus started yelling, "There's no water in the ocean!" Bunji continued, "Being that it was April first, April Fools' Day, half of us didn't believe what they were saying . . ."

But it was as true as it was strange. Nobody had ever seen anything like it—the ocean pulling so far back from shore. "You can imagine seeing that bare ocean floor in front of us, where there was usually ten to fifteen feet of deep water," Bunji said. "There were fish flopping around."

The withdrawn water exposed more than three hundred yards of ocean floor. Children could see wet rocks covered with what looked like bright red moss glistening in the morning light.

As students arrived at school, some of them hurried down to the shoreline to investigate. Giggling, curious children hopped across rocks to catch flopping fish in their bare hands. One handsome young science teacher led some of his high school students down to the seabed for a closer look at marine flora and fauna.

Ronald Yamaoka, a sixth grader, noticed the receding water as he walked to school. He remembered dropping off his books in his classroom and then running "down to the shore. And the kids were all there—you know, having a great time, thinking this was like a carnival or a show. . . . There were small pools, and I saw small fishes in the pools. These guys went down and tried to catch them. Suddenly, the older boys started yelling, 'Big wave, big wave!'"

FIRST WAVE

The first wave of the tsunami did not look like an artist's painting of a giant wave. It did not rear up into a curl, topped with a frothy whitecap. Instead, it just looked like a high wall made of water. A wall that roared as it approached the coast.

When the children realized that the water was going to slam into the land instead of stopping at the shoreline, they began to run. Terrified, some kids scrambled up the bleachers—the highest nearby structure. Others bolted for the school or nearby houses.

Clarence Ferdun, the school principal, described the first wave in a report written after the event: "At seven fifteen, I left my cottage and walked about forty yards to my office in the main school building. As I entered my office that faced the ocean, I saw a huge wall of water as high as the lighthouse on the point. Within seconds, the wave pushed against the seven teachers' cottages that were close to the shore . . . then raced through the coconut grove, across the park-playground, and under the main school building."

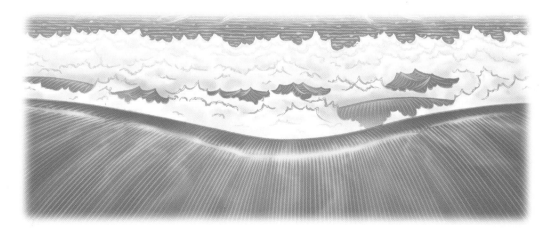

With incredible force, the water gushed over the land. Ronald Yamaoka said, "The wave hit my ankles and knocked me down. . . . Then the next thing I knew I was just tumbling in the lawn, in the yard. The wave inundated me. . . . I was treading water to keep my head above water, and it was like a flood. Dirty brown water just converged and then washed us out to sea."

OVER THE BRIM

After the first wave finally began pulling back to the sea, several children ran back to the shore. They thought the danger was over, but two larger waves were about to hit the peninsula.

The second big wave washed in. Again, it poured right past the shoreline and rushed across the school grounds, advancing onto higher and higher ground. The flooding lasted several minutes, and eyewitnesses said swirling water seemed to be coming from all directions at once. Others compared the churning water to a washing machine. Some children said it reminded them of how water looks when it's boiling on the stove.

Children who were caught by the wave grabbed for anything to keep them afloat. Some were swept into bushes or trees. They clung to the shaky branches, screaming for help. Others scrambled onto floating planks.

Bunji Fujimoto ran to higher ground when the first wave hit. From the road above the harbor, he watched the second and third waves cover the peninsula. He compared them to water filling a cup. "But when it reaches the brim, it doesn't stop. . . . I saw the bleachers collapse, like a house of matchsticks, and just fall apart. I can recall the big timber that they used for braces all falling apart, making terrifying cracking sounds. . . . It picked up a cottage like it was a little toy and slammed it through the trees."

Joseph Ah Choy, another teenager, also ran from the rushing water. When he looked back, he saw "one house going in the ocean all in pieces. . . . we [could] hear guys crying and yelling." Joseph described the wave hitting people and knocking them down, "like dominoes."

The third and largest wave at Laupahoehoe reared up like an angry tiger. As it swept onto the shore, the surge swamped people bobbing on makeshift rafts. By now, the water stunk of mud, oil, and other spilled substances. Heavy boulders of coral, sections of roofing, hunks of wall, porch railings, sofas, tables, and trees swirled in the turbulence. These objects rammed into stand-ing structures, causing even more damage. People were sucked under the churning water.

lighthouse

The tsunami waves that slammed into Laupahoehoe devastated most of the town. The lighthouse near the point of the peninsula, however, remained intact—until it was knocked down by high surf the following year.

Eighth-grader Everett Spencer ran away from the third wave. When he turned around, he saw a cottage floating on the water toward some rocks. Three teachers were on its roof. As he watched, the cottage slid under the water, and the teachers disappeared.

The horrible morning dragged on. There was no way to know if another giant wave was coming. The churning water was filled with large objects, making the surf far too dangerous for even the strongest of swimmers. People standing on high ground could see children floating on debris far out in the ocean. But the boats on the peninsula had all been destroyed or washed out to sea. Heartsick onlookers could only watch as stranded youngsters called and waved, dipping and rising on the swells.

Willie Choy Hee was doing construction work near the school that morning.

He remembered watching children float out to sea. "I tell you it was a pitiful sight . . . the kids out there on the lauhala branches . . . floating. Nothing you could do."

Principal Ferdun later wrote, "After the ocean had receded to its normal level, you could see people floating on wreckage offshore. The current was slowly taking them. . . . I called the police, the Coast Guard, the Navy, and everyone we could think of for help. They all told me they had all they could do with the problems in Hilo. . . . We would have to do the best we could to take care of our problems."

A TERRIBLE TOLL

When survivors were sure that the tsunami was over, they began to comb the shore for friends and family. Bunji Fujimoto found his older brother, but there was no sign of his younger brother. "We figured the small one was caught in the wave," he explained. Unfortunately, their guess was correct. The Fujimoto family "never saw or heard from him again."

Fifteen-year-old Yoshikazu "Kazu" Murakami was one of the few Laupahoehoe students who was washed out to sea during the tsunami and was later rescued. After Kazu had been in the water for almost thirty hours, sailors aboard a U. S. Navy transport ship spotted him. One of the sailors, David Cook, climbed down a cargo net and pulled the unconscious teenager from the water to the safety of the ship. In 2003, almost sixty years after the tsunami, Kazu and David officially met for the first time at the Pacific Tsunami Museum in Hilo after museum staff identified them as the boy and the rescuer in the photograph.

Hawaii ✠ Times

EXTRA!!!
TEEN SURVIVES TSUNAMI!

Tenth-grader Herbert Nishimoto stood on a small hill and watched the first and second waves wash onto the point. But the third wave was much higher. It kept coming right over the hill, and Herbert took off running. He tried to reach a friend's home. But just as he managed to get one leg over the porch railing, the house began tilting into the rushing water. In a split second, the stove came crashing toward him. Holding his hands over his head to shield himself, Herbert felt the house collapse, and he was dragged into the turbulent water.

He landed on a rocky reef. While he struggled out of his tight jeans, another wave arrived. He tried to dive under it, but one of his pants legs caught on the reef. Battered by the sharp rocks, Herbert expected to drown. His next memory was of floating in debris with sharks around him. A piece of flooring drifted by, and he scrambled onto it. As he bobbed in the ocean, he grabbed for logs and other debris. Using an axe handle that he found floating in the water as a tool and nails from broken boards, he pounded together a makeshift raft.

Herbert passed two other boys, one on a half-sunk barrel and another on a door. He pulled them aboard his raft. All three were worn-out from struggling against the wild water, but they had to keep alert. If their flimsy raft bumped into rocks and floating logs, it would break apart and dump them into the angry ocean. They realized the current was pulling them deeper out to sea, but what could they do?

Finally, in the afternoon, a seaplane dropped an inflatable raft to the boys, and they pulled themselves onto it. To ease their thirst, they drank the milk from coconuts floating in the water. No other help arrived, and the sun went down, leaving them alone in the dark. They dozed off, not knowing whether they would survive the night. By the next morning, the three had drifted ten miles south.

When the sun came up, they scanned the horizon for a rescue boat. But a boat never came, and they held on to their flimsy raft, knowing they were drifting farther and farther away from home. Just before noon, a girl on shore spotted the boys. Running to get help, she found some sugarcane workers on their lunch break. Two of the men were strong swimmers and managed to reach the exhausted boys and tow them to shore.

A Teacher's Miraculous Story

Marsue McGinnis and the three other teachers who shared her beachfront cottage were awakened by a student, who urged them to "come see the tidal wave." Still wearing their pajamas, the four teachers watched the first waves pour onto shore and recede. Marsue hurried into her bedroom to throw on some clothes. She grabbed her camera and hurried onto the porch to get a photo of this amazing event. When the third wave rushed in, it swamped the structure and swept Marsue into the sea. The other three teachers were also engulfed. One woman couldn't swim and was immediately dragged under. Marsue soon lost sight of the other two.

Marsue doesn't remember how or when her shoes and clothing were pulled off by the heaving water. She found herself "surrounded by rubbish, parts of boards . . . plants, trees. . . . I clung onto several boards that were still nailed together and kinda paddled around. . . . I thought, 'Every bone in my body is broken.'

"I saw a number of children floating near me, clinging to wreckage," she remembered. "We just kept floating out to sea, and some of the children disappeared."

Only one boat was available in the whole community of Laupahoehoe—a sailboat. By the time it could be fitted with an outboard motor, it was mid-afternoon. Just before darkness fell, rescuers finally reached Marsue, sixth-grader Ronald Yamoaka, and one other boy.

Marsue spent nine hours in the water before she was rescued. Of the four teachers who shared her cottage, she was the only one who survived. (Marsue's good luck continued after the event: One of the rescuers on the boat was a young doctor whom Marsue was dating. They eventually married.)

Marsue McGinnis with Dr. Leabert Fernandez at the Laupahoehoe Point Memorial ceremony on April 1, 1948

Frank DeCaires searched for three members of his family—his older brother and sister, as well as his younger adopted sister, Janet. Most of the people killed in Laupahoehoe were never found, but Janet's body was one of only three recovered. Her remains were found entangled in barbed wire and "all bruised up." Frank said she had "sand in the eyes, in the ears. It was like you took a pin hammer and just pounded."

Altogether, twenty-six people died in Laupahoehoe.

Sixteen of the victims were schoolchildren.

CHAPTER TWO

The Harbor of Hilo

Gigantic wave came crashing down,
People fled from all around.

The wave tore families apart,
Left friends with broken hearts.

RUN! RUN! RUN! as fast as you can,
*Don't look back! OH MAN! OH MAN!**

The three giant waves struck Laupahoehoe just as children were arriving for school. Because of this timing, many youngsters died—more than might have at another time of day.

But the April Fools' Day tsunami took even more lives in other places. In nearby Hilo, the shape of the harbor created a rebound effect, and giant waves washed into the town's harbor-front business district. Since it was so early in the morning, downtown stores were not yet open, so shoppers and merchants were not endangered. But the waves did claim the lives of many people who lived downtown.

*from a 1996 poem by fifth-grader Lenny Ambrosio, written as part of the Laupahoehoe School Oral History Project and published in *April Fools'...: The Laupahoehoe Tragedy of 1946, An Oral History.* Hawaii: Obun Hawaii, Inc., 1997.

TIGER WAVES

The greatest loss of life occurred in the Japanese neighborhood known as Shinmachi, or "New Town," along the Wailoa River and close to the harbor. In these closely packed buildings, many people were killed when their homes buckled. Although Shinmachi residents lived beside the water, many of them had never considered the danger of a tsunami.

Harold Tanouye, an eleven-year-old boy, was getting ready for school that morning. He heard a neighbor shouting what he thought were the words: "Tiger, tiger!"

Of course, the man was trying to warn his neighbors not of a tiger, but of an approaching "tidal wave." Although Harold did not understand the man's warning, he looked outside. Instead of a ferocious tiger, he saw people running from a ferocious wave!

Donald Nirei, age twelve, also lived in Shinmachi. He and his sixteen-year-old brother were getting ready for school when they heard someone yell, "Tsunami!" The brothers rushed to the front of their home and saw the wave coming. But by the time they reached their parents in the back of the house, water was already

People ran for their lives when they saw and heard the roaring tsunami waves gushing toward them.

ripping into the building. The family linked arms to stay together as their home caved in. But the surging water swept Donald's mother and father out the doorway and knocked the two brothers under the house. The boys managed to survive by scrambling onto a floating building. After the water receded, the brothers discovered their mother lying dead on a street. Four days later, they finally located their father when his body washed up on the beach. The tsunami turned Donald and his brother into orphans.

Is a "tsunami" the same as a "tidal wave"?

Some people still use the term "tidal wave" instead of the more accurate word "tsunami" for the unusual and sometimes deadly waves like the ones that smashed into Laupahoehoe and Hilo.

The word "tsunami" came into widespread use in the United States during the 1960s. It is a Japanese word that means "big harbor wave." Since Japan is the country that has experienced the most tsunamis, it makes sense for the Japanese word to be the accepted name.

"Tsunami" is also a more accurate name because these waves are *not* caused by tides. And, as the Japanese word implies, the deadliest effects of a tsunami usually occur in harbors.

Japanese kanji characters for "tsunami"

"The Great Wave" by Katsushika Hokusai (1760–1849) is sometimes incorrectly used to show a tsunami wave. It is actually an illustration of waves caused by the winds on the surface of the sea.

WASHED AWAY

Another Shinmachi teen, fourteen-year-old Yoshinobu Terada, had gone out early that morning to check on the family's boat, which was tied up along the Wailoa River. As soon as he saw it—still tied up but sitting on dry land—Yoshi knew something was terribly wrong. Quickly, he made for home, but a wave rushing through the alley was much faster. Yoshi jumped onto a neighbor's porch and through the open front door. Horrified, he realized that the back of the house was torn off! He could hear splintering wood all around him as the house began to fill with water and slide down the riverbank.

Yoshi desperately scanned the river and was astonished when his brother's surfboard came floating by. He leaped onto the board and hung on tight as it carried him up the river.

Yoshi was even more amazed when he spotted his mother on the riverbank. "She grabbed my hand and wouldn't let go," he said. Together, Yoshi and his mom watched the third wave wash in. Although they were about three-quarters of a mile from shore, a little water actually lapped their feet! Luckily, it was only six inches deep that far inland, so Yoshi's frightening experience with a tsunami finally came to an end.

Ten-year-old Matilda Moonie lived with her large, extended family in a house in Shinmachi. The first wave shook the building, and Matilda ran to grab her two younger brothers. But when the third wave swept into their home, it pulled Matilda into the swirling water and snatched her brothers out of her arms. Alone and scared, she caught a glimpse of her sister, grandmother, and an uncle as the water swept her away. She managed to climb onto a floating roof, but lost her balance and slipped back into the muddy water. A neighbor spotted Matilda in the debris and pulled her to safety.

Matilda's clothes were torn off, and she was badly bruised and swollen. The

In the Hawaiian language, two words are used to describe a tsunami. The first, "Kai e'e," is a word for the waves of the tsunami. A special word for the pulling back of the waters before the tsunami is "Kai mimiki."

neighbors cut up an old burlap bag as a makeshift dress for her. Later, when Matilda's mother came looking for her, she did not recognize her disfigured daughter at first. Although Matilda survived her ordeal, the tsunami proved tragic for her family: Three of her brothers, her grandmother, and an aunt drowned.

Toshio Fukuda was at work in a Hilo bakery when knee-high water poured over the sidewalk out front. The second wave pushed dirty water into the shop. Toshio and the other workers escaped and headed for a railroad station on higher ground. From this spot, Toshio could see Shinmachi. He saw a house flowing down the Wailoa River toward an approaching wave. Toshio recalled, "I saw a lady in the house yelling for help. So a fisherman ran with a long bamboo stick, but the bamboo stick couldn't reach her." The next thing Toshio saw was the house smashing into a bridge.

(right) Monster waves swelled as tall as coconut trees before pounding the shores of Hilo.

The Hilo waterfront was badly damaged.

A boat was washed four hundred feet inland.

A SAFE PLACE

Fortunately, one building in Shinmachi did withstand the force of the water. The Coca-Cola Bottling Plant, a concrete two-story building, saved the lives of many people who managed to reach it.

Seventeen-year-old Yasue Tsutsumi and her family were among the lucky ones. Before fleeing from their home, Yasue remembers standing on the family's veranda with her sister. The girls saw neighbors "floating up the river in their houses screaming for help."

When Yasue's family reached the bottling plant, they huddled together. Yasue remembered the sounds of the calamity:

Shinmachi Tsunami Memorial

"We could hear the roar of waves. It sounded like when you push something heavy . . . a rumbling sound and a roar."

WHAT CAUSED THE APRIL FOOLS' DAY TSUNAMI?

An underwater earthquake off the coast of the Aleutian Islands near Alaska is usually blamed for this tsunami. The steel-reinforced Scotch Cap Lighthouse, located in Alaska near the epicenter of the earthquake, was washed away by the initial wave. This lighthouse stood 138 feet tall, the height of a thirteen-story building. When the tsunami reached Hawaii, it created surges as high as forty-five feet.

The earthquake measured around 7.8 on the Richter Scale—a powerful quake, but by no means the most powerful quake recorded. How did this earthquake produce such a devastating tsunami? For years, scientists assumed the earthquake had triggered an underwater landslide. Together, the earthquake and landslide would have created enough force to generate the deadly April Fools' Day tsunami. But in 2004, the Scripps Institute of Oceanography studied the seafloor.

Gerard Fryer, a professor at the University of Hawaii, said, "We found no landslide where there should have been a landslide. I was stunned."

So what *did* cause this deadly tsunami? Scientists are still investigating. Some believe the earthquake was more powerful than recorded. Seismographs in the 1940s could accurately measure only one type of earthquake—the type that produces a rapid movement of the earth. Back then, slower-moving quakes tended to register false, low-magnitude readings.

The Scotch Cap Lighthouse before the tsunami *The ruins of the lighthouse after the tsunami*

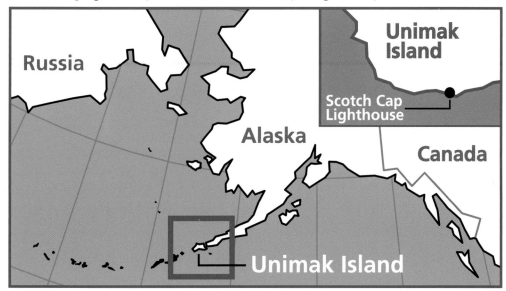

The Cost of the Tsunami: Hawaii and Beyond

Ninety-six people were killed in the town of Hilo during the 1946 tsunami. During the cleanup after the disaster, workers gathered the dead and delivered the corpses to the Dodo Mortuary. Since there were more corpses than the building could hold, the workers lined the bodies along the street. Some of the corpses awaiting burial had to be stored in an icehouse.

The downtown business district was demolished, as was the local railroad. Almost five hundred homes and businesses were destroyed, and a thousand more were damaged. Bridges, roads, ships, and cars were wrecked. The estimated total of the city's property damage was about twenty-six million dollars in 1946; translated into today's dollars, the damage amounted to more than 260 million dollars!

The April Fools' Day tsunami killed people in other places besides Hilo and Laupahoehoe. Altogether, 159 people died across all of the Hawaiian Islands. Of that number, forty-four bodies were never recovered. The tsunami also killed six Americans who were thousands of miles from Hawaii: Five Coast Guardsmen manning a lighthouse

The Okino Hotel was among the many buildings in Hilo destroyed by the tsunami.

in Alaska were killed when a one-hundred-foot wave swept away their building. Another person drowned off the coast of California.

But reports of the number of people killed and the cost of property damage do not capture the personal impact of such a disaster. Imagine how teenager

Yasue Matsui felt when she learned that her high school friend, Tomie Izumi, had "died instantly when she was struck on the bridge of the nose by a beam of lumber." Searching for Tomie's body, Yasue went to the Dodo Mortuary and "saw all those bodies wrapped in burlap bags." Years later, she still remembered the horrible sight.

At the end of that school year, the *Blue and Gold*, Hilo High School's yearbook, was dedicated to "quiet and unassuming" Tomie Izumi, the member of the class of '46 who "lost her life in the tidal wave." As Yasue said, "Poor Tomie! She didn't get married. She didn't get a job. So sad! She was a sweet girl."

Is a tsunami a single, giant wave?

No, a tsunami is a series of waves—sometimes ten or more. The waves may follow each other at five-minute intervals, or they may be spaced as much as an hour-and-a-half apart. The series is sometimes called the "tsunami wave train."

Which wave will be the largest? Nobody can predict. Each tsunami is unique. Sometimes a fairly small wave is followed by larger waves. Other times, the first wave is the largest.

Hawaii

The
Ring of Fire

CHAPTER THREE

Deadly History

Tsunami waves can be towering, destructive monsters. Or they can be no higher than the usual wind waves that lap most shorelines. In Hawaii, monstrous tsunami waves—those that kill people and destroy homes, like the waves that struck Laupahoehoe and Hilo—have always been part of island history. Destructive tsunamis are described in ancient island legends. They became part of Hawaii's written records during the 1800s.

The first deadly tsunami in Hawaii's recorded history took place in 1837. Two missionaries—one in Hilo and another on the island of Maui—recorded the details. In Hilo, Reverend Titus Coan told of "a gigantic wave . . . rushing in with the rapidity of a racehorse" that caused as much destruction "as if a heavy mountain had fallen on the beach." In Maui, missionary Richard Armstrong described how an entire village—people, houses, livestock, and boats—was picked up and swept eight hundred feet inland and into a lake by a wall of ocean water!

In 1868, two powerful tsunamis struck the islands within a few months, in April and again in August. Nine years later, another tsunami killed five people in Hilo and destroyed thirty-seven houses. In 1923, a fisherman was killed in Hilo Bay by a tsunami that damaged the railway, wharves, and some houses.

The April Fools' Day tsunami was not the last deadly tsunami in Hawaii's history. In 1960—only fourteen years later—a very powerful earthquake in Chile triggered a tsunami that killed sixty-one Hawaiians and demolished downtown Hilo again. This time, property damage amounted to about 320 million dollars (calculated in today's dollars).

Altogether, nearly three hundred Hawaiians have been killed by tsunamis since records have been kept. The tsunami death toll for inhabitants of this Pacific paradise exceeds that caused by earthquakes, volcanoes, and hurricanes, *combined*.

TSUNAMIS IN AMERICA AND AROUND THE WORLD

Hawaii is not the only place where American lives are threatened by tsunamis. In fact, more Americans have been killed by tsunamis than by earthquakes during the last fifty years. Earthquakes off Alaska triggered three major Pacific-wide tsunamis during the last century, as well as the landslide that produced the highest tsunami wave ever recorded (seventeen hundred feet!) in Lituya Bay during the local tsunami of 1958.

In the "lower forty-eight" states, tsunamis have also claimed lives. In 1964, when a tsunami struck Crescent City, California, eleven people were killed, and the business district was destroyed. This tsunami claimed the lives of four campers on a beach in Newport, Oregon, as well.

In addition to the death toll on American shores, Americans have also been killed by tsunamis that struck foreign shores when they were visiting abroad.

America is not the only country that has lost lives to tsunamis. In fact, of all the countries in the world, Japan has experienced the greatest number of destructive tsunamis. In the terrible tsunami of 1896, about twenty-five thousand Japanese were killed. During the last thirteen hundred years—all the years that records have been kept—tsunamis have killed approximately sixty-six thousand Japanese inhabitants.

Japan is an island nation, and Hawaii is an island state. Both of them, as well as Alaska and California, have coasts along the Pacific Ocean, where about nine out of ten tsunamis have formed. During recorded history, about 140,000 people have been killed by tsunamis in the Pacific Ocean.

What causes tsunamis?

Scientists think most Hawaiian tsunamis—like most major tsunamis around the world—are caused by large undersea earthquakes. When an earthquake occurs in the seabed under the ocean, the thrust of the ocean floor can move a large mass of water. From the earthquake's origin (or "epicenter"), the water ripples outward, just as it does when you hold your fist under the surface of your bathwater and suddenly thrust it upward.

What causes earthquakes? Just as an egg is covered by a thin shell, the earth is covered by a crust of rock. This crust is cracked into gigantic pieces, called "plates." These are named *tectonic plates*, from the Greek word for "architect" or "builder," because the movement of these sheets of rock is the major force that shapes the land on Earth. How thick is the earth's crust? It varies. Under continents, the plates of rock may extend as much as a hundred miles below the surface. But under the ocean, the thickness may only be about nine miles. (The average thickness of all the earth's tectonic plates is between forty and fifty miles.)

Although the earth's crust seems firm and solid, these plates of rock are actually moving. They float on molten magma, a fluid material that resembles hot pudding. The movement is very slow, no faster than the speed at which fingernails grow. When these plates of rock slam into each other—or suddenly slip loose from interlocking with each other—they cause a jolt, or earthquake. The earthquake is actually a shockwave that moves through the earth's crust and shakes the ground.

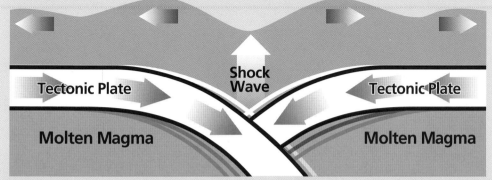

When tectonic plates suddenly shift or collide in the seabed under the ocean, a shockwave pushes water away from the plate movement's epicenter. If the shockwave is strong enough, the ripple motion of the water can produce powerful tsunami waves.

But these disasters also happen in other oceans. Scientists estimate that nearly a quarter of the world's people live in areas that have some possibility of experiencing a tsunami.

People living on the coasts of the Atlantic Ocean have also experienced powerful tsunamis. In 1755, a very strong earthquake in Lisbon, Portugal, caused a tsunami that raced across the Atlantic Ocean and hit both North Africa and the Caribbean. More than sixty thousand people were killed.

Although Indian Ocean tsunamis do not happen as frequently as those in the Pacific, some of the deadliest have occurred in this region. In 1883, the Krakatoa volcano, located on a small island between Sumatra and Java, erupted. This event has been called the "catastrophe of the century" because its effects were felt around the world. The eruption lasted several weeks and triggered several tsunamis. The largest tsunami wiped out the entire population of a small nearby island, as well as thousands of people living near Indonesian shores. The death toll exceeded forty thousand.

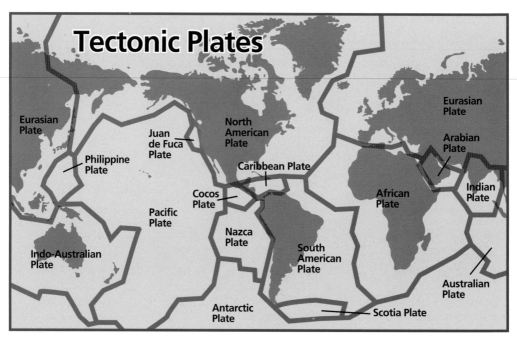

Tectonic Plates

Eurasian Plate

Eurasian Plate

Juan de Fuca Plate

North American Plate

Arabian Plate

Philippine Plate

Caribbean Plate

Indian Plate

Cocos Plate

African Plate

Pacific Plate

Nazca Plate

South American Plate

Indo-Australian Plate

Australian Plate

Antarctic Plate

Scotia Plate

Black Sunday, 2004

Far more deadly than the one caused by the eruption of Krakatoa was the tsunami that formed in the Indian Ocean the morning after Christmas 2004. This was one of the worst natural disasters of all time. The exact number of lives lost will probably never be known, because the tsunami wiped away every trace of whole villages—houses, businesses, roads, and people. The United Nations estimates that this disaster claimed the lives of more than 223,000 people! Besides the dead, the tsunami injured countless people. More than two million people became homeless, and one-and-a-half million lost their

Tsunami waves wash ashore on Phi Phi Island, Thailand, on December 26, 2004.

livelihoods. More than a dozen countries were directly affected by this disaster.

An extremely powerful earthquake (with a magnitude between 9.1 and 9.3 on the Richter Scale), the fourth strongest in history, triggered this tsunami. It occurred near Indonesia and lasted four minutes. The quake's epicenter was underwater, west of the northern tip of the Indonesian island of Sumatra. During the shaking, buildings collapsed, and people were killed in the city of Banda Aceh, a provincial capital at the northern end of Sumatra. But the worst effects were yet to come.

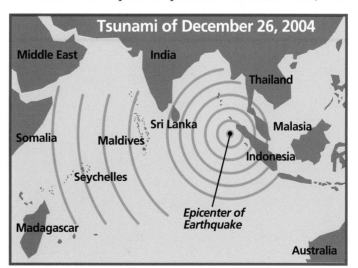

Tsunami of December 26, 2004

Middle East
India
Thailand
Somalia
Sri Lanka
Malasia
Maldives
Indonesia
Seychelles
Epicenter of Earthquake
Madagascar
Australia

What caused this quake? The subduction of the Indo-Australian Plate. Over centuries, this giant raft of rock has been gradually subducting, or sliding below, the Eurasian Plate (below Indonesia), but this movement of tectonic plates is not a smooth process. As the gigantic Indo-Australian slab inched under its neighbor, the two plates got stuck, and the Eurasian Plate was pulled down. When it suddenly snapped loose on the morning of December 26, 2004, it released more energy than twenty thousand atom bombs—that's enough energy to boil forty gallons of water for each person on Earth! It actually released so much energy that it sped up the spin of our planet—temporarily shortening the length of our days by a teeny, tiny fraction of a second—and made Earth wobble, just as an imbalanced tire produces a wobble in a car.

The snapping motion of the Eurasian Plate lifted the seabed forty feet or higher along a rupture line of about six hundred miles, displacing billions of tons of water. Because the earthquake's rupture ran north and south, most of the water surged east and west of the fault line.

The northern end of Sumatra was nearest to the epicenter, so this island got the first and worst of the waves. About fifteen minutes after the quake, tsunami waves taller than coconut trees began slamming into the shores of Banda Aceh. A flood of water eight to twelve feet deep covered the city. During the flooding, buildings were plowed into rubble by mounds of wet

How often do tsunamis happen?

Around the world, about one hundred tsunamis are detected each year, but very few of these cause any damage. On average, every year about twelve of these tsunamis form large enough waves to cause any property damage, injuries, or deaths.

Along the Pacific Coast of the continental United States (including Alaska), about six tsunamis per year are detected, and only two of these will cause any damage or injury. In Hawaii, tsunami records have been kept since 1813. Since that time, Hawaii has had ninety-five tsunamis, an average of one tsunami every other year.

debris moving between ten and thirty miles per hour.

Camera operator Geoff Mackley visited Banda Aceh after the disaster. "I've been to more than thirty hurricanes and thirty-five volcanic eruptions," he said, "so I . . . thought I'd seen everything nature could throw up. But . . . this is . . . beyond belief . . . like the aftermath of an atomic bomb, maybe worse."

Tsunami waves quickly flooded coastal villages. After the tsunami, all that remained of many villages was one or two buildings and piles of debris.

About three-fourths of all the people killed by the tsunami lived on Sumatra.

As tsunami waves swept outwards from the earthquake's undersea rupture, water slammed into the nearby Andaman and Nicobar Islands, killing more than seven thousand islanders. In Burma, nearly one hundred people were killed.

One hour after the earthquake, tsunami waves reached southern Thailand to the east. Monstrous walls of water swamped beach resorts and coastal towns. More than five thousand residents, as well as vacationers from thirty-seven countries, were killed. An American vacationer staying at a Thai resort saw her beach bungalow collapse around her. She said, "It was like a truck crashed through the wall." Even more people were killed when the waves reached Malaysia.

Tourists from many countries were killed when the tsunami hit beaches and coastal towns where they were staying. Lifeguards on this beach at a hotel in Malaysia saw the huge waves and quickly sounded a warning for everyone to run to the safety area.

Meanwhile, the tsunami was also moving west. Waves hammered Sri Lanka, an island nation off the coast of India. This small country's death toll exceeded thirty thousand, and about forty percent of them were children. Along Sri Lanka's southern coast, the rushing water derailed a passenger train, the *Queen of the Sea Express*. About one thousand people were killed, making this the world's worst rail disaster. One of the survivors remembered the tsunami as "a wall of water . . . the sky was blocked." A train guard managed to rescue some of the passengers. He said the wave looked alive, "like a big monster! It had a black

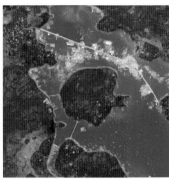

Flooding caused by the tsunami reshaped entire landscapes, as shown in these before and after satellite photos of the Aceh Besar district in Aceh, Sumatra.

mouth and white head and was trying to eat us." Waves also struck the coast of India, claiming some ten thousand more lives.

Seven hours after the earthquake's eruption, the tsunami hit the east coast of Africa with still enough power that it killed people in four more countries.

During this colossal tsunami, the height of the waves varied from place to place because of differences in the shape of the shorelines. A wave taller than ninety feet was recorded on the Indian Ocean side of Sumatra. In some places, water flooded inland as far as four miles. Coastlines were actually reshaped by the astounding power of the waves.

In just a few hours, the tsunami caused such incredible destruction that experts claim it will take decades to completely rebuild all of the damaged communities. One year after the disaster, about sixty thousand people were still living in tents because they had no homes. The total cost reached the billions. The United States alone gave 1.6 billion dollars to tsunami victims.

Even though that is an enormous amount of destruction, buildings are easier to rebuild than lives. In Banda Aceh, so many corpses were left in the wake of the tsunami that more than fifty thousand unidentified bodies had to be placed into a mass grave in a field. Grieving relatives live with the knowledge that they were not able to bury their loved ones with traditional respect or dignity. Indeed, they will probably never know which bodies were buried in that grave. In Banda Aceh, the city hardest hit by both the earthquake and resulting tsunami, survivors remember December 26, 2004, as "Black Sunday."

An Ancient Mystery

Plato

For many years, historians and scientists have wondered: Did a tsunami cause the disappearance of the "Lost Civilization of Atlantis"?

Atlantis was an island-nation described two thousand years ago by a famous ancient Greek philosopher named Plato. According to Plato's tale, Atlantis was wealthy, powerful, and technologically advanced. He described its citizens as fair-minded and hardworking— at first, that is. But they became greedy and corrupt. To punish them for their selfishness, the gods unleashed the sea. In an instant, water swallowed Atlantis, leaving no trace of its citizens or its culture. To this day, no one knows if Plato invented the story of Atlantis to teach a lesson or if his tale was based on an actual place and a real event.

Some archaeologists believe that Atlantis was a real island located near Crete in the Aegean Sea. Geologists have found evidence of a volcanic eruption that occurred in 1470 BC, which triggered a tsunami in the Aegean Sea. This tsunami could have swept away an entire island, as in Plato's story. If this speculation is correct, then a tsunami actually erased a civilization!

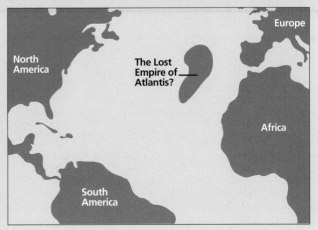

A Gift of the Tsunami

Occasionally, a tsunami will deliver an unexpected gift. Ten days after the December 2004 tsunami in the Indian Ocean, villagers in a small fishing village in southeastern India spotted a raft bobbing along the shore. When they pulled it in, they discovered a nine-inch-tall brass statue—a smiling figure, the likeness of a Buddhist sage. The statue had drifted more than one thousand miles, all the way from Burma.

Even more surprising was the discovery made by villagers in the nearby Indian town of Mahabalipuram. The receding water temporarily exposed surprises on the ocean floor. As the tsunami approached, they got a glimpse of what had been the temples of a mythical city! One local merchant said, "We stared in awe, and then we ran for our lives." Archaeologists believe the temples are six of the mythical seven pagodas, part of a seventh-century port city that was described

Among the treasures revealed by the tsunami on the Mahabalipuram coast were ancient sculptures that had been carved into boulders. Some of the sculptures depicted animals, such as the elephant and lion above. Most were of lions, symbols of the ruling family who had built the temples at Mahabalipuram.

more than two hundred years ago by a British tourist. According to local myth, this large city was so beautiful that the jealous gods sent a flood to swallow most of it. (The seventh temple, still on dry land, is a famous tourist destination.)

Along the beach of the same town, tsunami waves washed away the sand that had buried carvings of tigers, elephants, horses, and other figures. Looking at the ancient stone carvings, a student said, "We used to come here many times, but we never saw these before. It is a gift of the tsunami."

The 2004 tsunami was not the only time ancient treasures have been revealed by giant waves. In 1960, a tsunami uncovered one of the most spectacular statues on Easter Island, the small island in the Pacific Ocean that is famous for its enormous carvings of human heads.

(top) The tsunami waves also exposed useful objects, such as stairways and water tanks, that had been carved into boulders.

(right) Mysterious head carvings on Easter Island

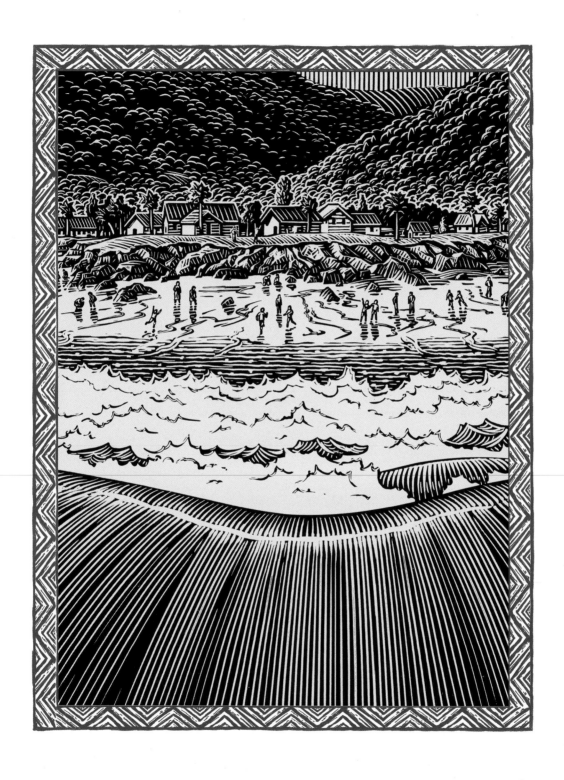

CHAPTER FOUR

Tsunami Science

After the 1946 April Fools' Day disaster, people around the world heard about the giant waves that poured over a schoolyard in Laupahoehoe and took the lives of children. News reports about the death and destruction in Hilo taught a terrible lesson: Tsunamis are deadly threats. Scientists became determined to find a way to protect people.

A group of oceanographers were conducting a meeting (about the Bikini atomic bomb tests) in Hawaii when the 1946 tsunami struck. These scientists saw firsthand the disastrous effects of the April Fools' Day tsunami. As a result, it became the most studied tsunami in history. A year later, three of the scientists published an article calling for a warning system that would save lives. They recommended that observation stations be built on Pacific Ocean coastal cities and islands. When these stations detected the large, long waves of a tsunami, they would immediately report the information to a central bureau. There the data would be analyzed and a warning sent to people in the path of the tsunami waves.

Actually, a tsunami warning system was not a new idea. It had been proposed before, but most people did not believe it would work. Why not?

Predicting Tsunamis

A tsunami moving through the open ocean is difficult to spot. Out at sea, a tsunami wave is barely measurable on the surface as a slight rise, no more than a foot or two. As it passes under ships, people on board assume it is merely another ocean swell. From an airplane, a tsunami on the open sea looks like a thin shadow-line moving swiftly across the surface of the water. That's why people usually don't recognize a tsunami until it gets closer to land.

Before the first tsunami wave hits the coast, the water may retreat from the shore and expose the ocean floor. When the sea runs backward like this, it gives a brief warning to people on the beach. If onlookers understand what they are seeing, they have a few minutes to move inland.

But some tsunamis do not begin with the water drawing back from shore. And if authorities wait until they notice the water retreating or until they can see the tsunami wave approaching, it's too late to issue a widespread warning. Tsunamis move fast. Their speed depends on the depth of the water they are traveling through—the deeper the water, the faster they move. In deep water, tsunamis travel as fast as jet planes. Although they begin to slow down when they reach the shallow ocean bottom surrounding land, the waves flood inland at the speed of a moving car: forty miles per hour or faster. To give people along the coast enough time to evacuate, a warning must be issued well before a tsunami is spotted approaching the shore.

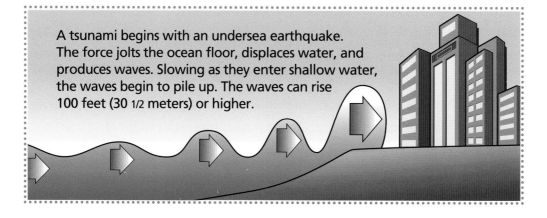

A tsunami begins with an undersea earthquake. The force jolts the ocean floor, displaces water, and produces waves. Slowing as they enter shallow water, the waves begin to pile up. The waves can rise 100 feet (30 1/2 meters) or higher.

If scientists could forecast when a tsunami would form, they could give people plenty of time to evacuate coastal areas at risk. Why is this event so difficult to predict? Most tsunamis are caused by earthquakes—and earthquakes are very common events. More than a million small earthquakes occur every year. It takes a powerful earthquake to produce a tsunami—usually one with a magnitude higher than 7.0 on the Richter Scale. But even powerful earthquakes are fairly common events. More than once a month, an earthquake powerful enough to cause a tsunami happens somewhere on Earth. In order to predict when a tsunami will form, scientists need to know which of these earthquakes will trigger tsunamis.

Can tsunamis be triggered by other causes?

Yes, tsunamis can also be triggered by "point sources," such as the eruption of volcanoes and landslides into bodies of water. A point source does not produce as much energy as the long rupture line of an earthquake. When a volcanic eruption or landslide starts a tsunami, it usually strikes only nearby shores. But these "local tsunamis" reach land quickly and may form gigantic waves, so they can be deadly and destructive. The highest tsunami wave ever recorded was at Lituya Bay, Alaska, and it was caused by a point source—a landslide.

Lituya Bay, Alaska, after the July 8, 1958 tsunami

How much do scientists know about earthquakes? Although earthquakes have always been part of life on Earth, people have only understood their cause for a few hundred years. The science of earthquakes, called "seismology," was first developed in the 1700s. During the next century, scientists collected information about quakes and began to make "seismographs," devices that measure their strength. Nowadays, earthquakes—even small ones—can be detected and measured with accuracy.

Scientists are able to predict that the pressures created by shifting tectonic plates will cause an earthquake in a general area. But they are not yet able to say exactly when it will happen, exactly where it will occur, or how strong it will be.

Professor Thomas Jaggar established the Hawaii Volcano Observatory in 1912. He was one of the first scientists to investigate the relationship between earthquakes and tsunamis. He was also one of the first to try to warn people about a tsunami. In 1923, Jaggar issued a tsunami warning in Hawaii after his seismograph recorded an earthquake off Alaska's Aleutian Islands. Unfortunately, people ignored his warning, and the resulting tsunami waves in Hilo Bay killed one fisherman and damaged property. But ten years later, in 1933, the Observatory issued another tsunami warning—and this time it *did* save lives.

From studying past tsunamis, scientists know that most tsunamis form when a strong earthquake happens under the sea. These undersea quakes are often "silent." People may not feel the ground shake as they do when a strong earthquake happens on land. Today, scientists have instruments that can detect undersea earthquakes.

Student Gets A+ for Tsunami Lesson

Tilly Smith, a ten-year-old girl from England, was vacationing in Thailand with her parents and little sister when the tsunami struck on December 26, 2004. She said she "was on the beach and the water started to go funny. There were bubbles and the tide went out all of a sudden. I recognized what was happening and had a feeling there was going to be a tsunami. I told Mummy."

About a hundred tourists hurried off the beach with the Smith family. Minutes later, a fifteen-foot wave washed onto the shore. According to Tilly's mom, the water "demolished everything in its path."

How did Tilly realize a tsunami was coming? She remembered a lesson that had been taught in her school's geography class!

Tilly Smith

So why don't scientists broadcast tsunami warnings whenever an undersea earthquake occurs? Because even a powerful undersea earthquake might not trigger a tsunami. Very powerful earthquakes are sometimes caused by sideways movements of tectonic plates, such as the horizontal motion of the plates grinding alongside California's famous San Andreas Fault. This motion produced the earthquake that devastated the city and surrounding areas in the Great San Francisco Disaster of 1906. But such sideways movement does not usually produce a major tsunami.

Certain types of earthquakes, however, are more likely to start a tsunami. Usually, these are powerful undersea quakes caused by one tectonic plate slipping under another one. These subduction earthquakes are the likely cause of most major tsunamis. When tectonic plates subduct, the ocean floor may snap

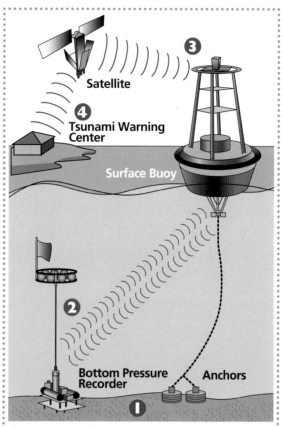

Tsunameters help scientists predict tsunamis and are set up in areas in the ocean where tsunamis are likely to be generated. Each tsunameter has two parts: a Bottom Pressure Recorder (BPR) and a surface buoy that is anchored to the ocean floor. The BPR measures changes in water pressure near the ocean floor and then transmits the data to the surface buoy above (1 and 2). The buoy has an antenna that allows a satellite to then gather the information and transmit it back down to scientists at tsunami warning centers all over the world (3 and 4). All of this is done in "real time," which means that scientists can see what's happening at the exact time it occurs.

up or drop down. This sudden thrust moves a huge amount of water, forming a tsunami. Every earthquake produces shockwaves. If it happens on land, the shockwaves travel through the Earth's crust, causing various kinds of changes and damage. If the quake happens on the seafloor, the shockwaves may become a tsunami moving through the water.

What Is the Ring of Fire?

The countries bordering the Pacific Ocean are sometimes called the Pacific Rim nations. On the map below, you can almost envision a "ring" that encircles the Pacific Ocean. Because this region experiences more strong earthquakes and volcanoes than any other place on Earth, it is nicknamed the "Ring of Fire."

Why does the Ring of Fire have so many earthquakes and volcanoes? Below the Pacific Ocean lies the Pacific Plate. Like all of Earth's tectonic plates, this huge slab is moving, pushing against the plates on either side of it. But in this region,

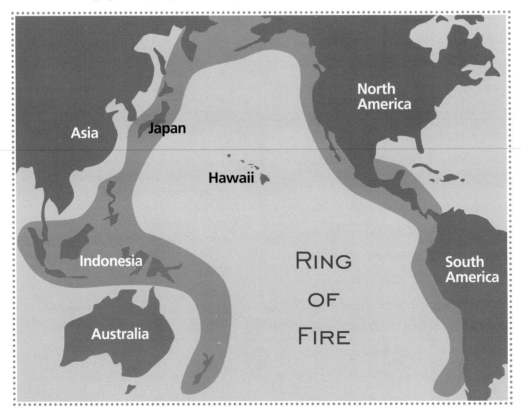

the tectonic plates tend to *subduct*—that is, they move over or under each other rather than grind against each other sideways. Subduction zones usually produce the greatest number of volcanoes and the most powerful earthquakes. When these earthquakes lift or drop sections of the ocean floor, they set off tsunamis.

THE ANATOMY OF TSUNAMI WAVES

Most ocean waves are shaped by the wind. Even during fierce storms, these wind waves are only made of surface water and rarely extend below five hundred feet. Wind waves travel fairly slowly—never faster than sixty miles per hour.

In contrast, tsunami waves are made of an entire water column from the ocean bottom all the way to its surface. That's the reason tsunami waves contain a huge volume of water—much more than wind waves.

Tsunami waves can travel at amazing speeds of up to six hundred miles per hour! Their speed is determined by the water's depth rather than the strength of the earthquake that triggered them. The deeper the water the tsunami travels through, the faster it moves.

Tsunami waves are much longer than wind waves. From crest to crest, wind waves are usually shorter than one thousand feet. But a tsunami wave may stretch one hundred miles from crest to crest. As a tsunami wave approaches a coast, its front edge begins to slow down because the ocean becomes shallower as it nears land. The back of the wave is still moving fast, so the water piles up and creates a giant wall of water that rushes onto shore.

The shape of the coastline, as well as its depth, can affect the size of a tsunami wave. Tsunami waves are usually higher along shallow coastlines than along

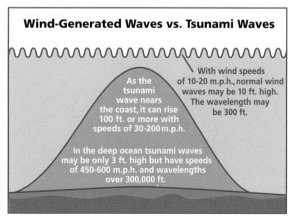

Wind-Generated Waves vs. Tsunami Waves

With wind speeds of 10-20 m.p.h., normal wind waves may be 10 ft. high. The wavelength may be 300 ft.

As the tsunami wave nears the coast, it can rise 100 ft. or more with speeds of 30-200 m.p.h.

In the deep ocean tsunami waves may be only 3 ft. high but have speeds of 450-600 m.p.h. and wavelengths over 300,000 ft.

coasts with deep drop-offs. Offshore islands and coral reefs, as well as trees or dense vegetation, may reduce the power of a tsunami wave when it strikes the mainland. All of these factors make the height of the waves on a particular coast difficult to predict. Sometimes towering tsunami waves will strike a harbor, but the coastal areas just a few miles away will receive much smaller waves.

Today, scientists use computers and wave pools to study tsunamis. These models are good at showing how tsunamis form, how large they will be, and where they will travel. At Oregon State University, scientists use a wave pool half as big as a football field to model the effects of tsunamis. This is the largest tank in the world devoted solely to tsunami research. Researchers flood miniature coastlines with tsunami waves to study their effects.

In addition to the wave pool, researchers at Oregon State University also use a large wave flume to measure the effects of tsunamis.

Because tsunamis are so dangerous, shouldn't people at the coast be evacuated whenever an undersea earthquake happens?

Most undersea earthquakes don't produce tsunamis, so it would not be practical to evacuate coastal communities each time an earthquake occurs. If too many tsunami warnings prove to be false alarms, most people will lose faith in the system and ignore future warnings.

Choosing to evacuate an area is a serious decision. In the past, during the rush to leave, people have been injured and killed. Evacuations are also expensive. One tsunami expert estimated that the price tag for an evacuation in Hawaii would be more than fifty million dollars! Why so expensive? Business comes to a halt during an evacuation. Emergency staff, such as police, firefighters, and road crews, must work overtime to divert traffic and establish shelters. Frequent evacuations can also leave a place with a bad reputation. If tourists are evacuated from a vacation area, they might stay away from seaside resorts, and this would hurt the economy by putting hotels, restaurants, and other attractions out of business.

The December 2004 Indian Ocean tsunami hits Ao Nang, Thailand.

U.S. Mainland at Risk: Cascadia

Scientists have pinpointed one area in the United States mainland where a deadly tsunami is likely to happen. This area lies along the coast of Oregon and Washington in a region called Cascadia. Major cities like Seattle, Washington, would be threatened by a tsunami in this area.

Here, the Juan de Fuca Plate (a fairly small tectonic plate sandwiched between the North American Plate and the Pacific Plate) meets the western side of the plate on which North America sits. This area is a subduction zone, similar to the area off Sumatra, where an earthquake triggered the 2004 Indian Ocean tsunami.

In Cascadia, the subducting plates have already caused at least seven earthquakes during the last thirty-five hundred years. Each earthquake was between three hundred and one thousand years apart. Cascadia's last earthquake was in 1700—about three hundred years ago. Did it cause a tsunami? Yes. A tsunami struck the northwest coast of the United States and traveled across the Pacific Ocean, hitting Hawaii, Japan, and Australia.

Scientists are warning that another earthquake in Cascadia could happen at any time. And when it does, coastal residents should be prepared to deal with a colossal tsunami.

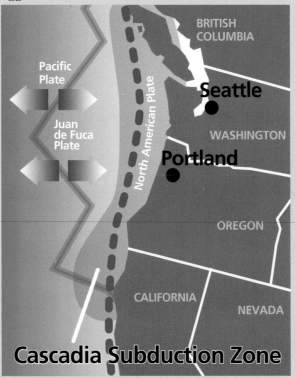

Extending from northern California to British Columbia, the Juan de Fuca Plate is being pushed underneath, or subducted by, the North American Plate at a rate of forty to fifty millimeters per year (mm/yr). Additional seismic activity exists further offshore originating from the Pacific Plate and the Juan de Fuca Plate spreading apart from each other.

SOME WARNING IS BETTER THAN NONE

Scientists have learned a lot of valuable information by studying wave pools, computer models, and past tsunamis. During the 2004 Indian Ocean tsunami, a NASA Oceanographic Satellite happened to be passing over the tsunami as it moved across the open sea. The satellite recorded the form of the tsunami waves and confirmed scientific theories that were originally based only on models.

In spite of all this information, scientists will not be able to predict when a tsunami will form until they can predict exactly when and where an earthquake will occur and how powerful it will be.

So how can people be protected from deadly tsunamis? How can the thousands of people who live on, work at, and visit coastal areas be safely removed from harm's way when a tsunami is detected? Authorities assumed for many years that a tsunami warning system would not work, but in spite of their reservations, a warning system was created for the Pacific Ocean after the 1946 April Fools' Day tragedy. More than half a century has passed since its creation, and during these years, scientists from many countries have cooperated to make the warning system better and faster. Although the Pacific Tsunami Warning System is still not perfect, it certainly has saved lives.

CHAPTER FIVE

Sound the Warning!

Two years after the April Fools' Day tsunami taught the world a deadly lesson, the United States launched its first tsunami warning center. The Pacific Tsunami Warning Center (PTWC) began operation in 1948.

Over the years, the PTWC has refined its methods and improved its technology. The center is now supported by twenty-six member countries, including Australia, Canada, Chile, China, and Japan, and it issues tsunami warnings around the Pacific. These warnings save lives.

How Does the PTWC Work?

Scientists with the National Oceanic and Atmospheric Administration (NOAA) operate warning centers in Hawaii and Alaska. They receive information from instruments placed around the Pacific Ocean.

In the early years, these scientists collected information from tide gauges that recorded near-shore water depths. The experts compared the data with reports of earthquakes from the National Earthquake Information Center in Golden, Colorado. Whenever an earthquake of magnitude 6.5 or greater was detected,

NOAA began investigating. If a tsunami seemed likely, they sent out warnings. But most of their warnings proved to be false alarms. At first, the scientists didn't have precise enough data to make their predictions.

Today, more accurate instruments have helped refine the warning system. In 2002, six pressure sensors were installed on the Pacific seabed. They monitor the depth of water. A change might indicate that a tsunami is passing over them. The sensors relay their data to large buoys floating on the water's surface. From the buoys, data is transmitted by satellite to the warning centers.

In addition to monitoring earthquake activity and water depth, today's scientists rely on computer models to predict tsunamis. These models are based on information learned from past earthquakes and from wave pools in the laboratory. The

How can water do so much damage?

Although water seems soft and light to the touch, it is actually very heavy. If you could cut a square block of water that measured a meter (about three feet) on each side, it would weigh a ton—as much as a car! During a powerful tsunami, such as the 2004 Indian Ocean tsunami, one hundred thousand tons of water can hit every five feet of the coastline. This astounding volume of water rushes inland at the speed of a moving bus. No wonder the Black Sunday tsunami did so much damage!

In addition to the incredible force of the water, a tsunami wave picks up sand and coral boulders and slams them against the shore. As buildings break apart, the retreating water sucks them out to sea, along with trees and cars and everything else in its path, including people. The next wave rams these objects against the coast. Just as a tornado picks up objects and hurtles them into houses and cars, a tsunami becomes even more deadly as it progresses.

Two ships that were washed inland at the waterfront of an industrial area near Banda Aceh, Sumatra, Indonesia, on December 26, 2004

How deep is the ocean?

The ocean's depth varies from place to place, with an average depth of more than twelve thousand feet—more than two miles deep. Near the edges of continents, an ocean may be relatively shallow, less than five hundred feet deep. Out at sea, the depth ranges from thirteen thousand to twenty thousand feet. But the Mariana Trench in the Pacific seafloor, the deepest section of ocean in the world, is more than thirty-six thousand feet deep—nearly seven miles.

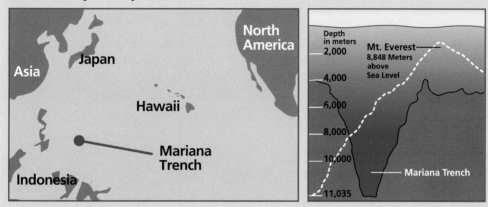

computer models calculate tsunami behavior based on the depths of the Pacific Ocean in various places and the shape of coastlines. As soon as seismographs detect a strong earthquake, scientists begin running computer programs to analyze the information. In a matter of minutes, they can make a fairly reliable prediction about whether a tsunami will form and how it will behave. Immediately, they broadcast warnings to coastal areas that are threatened.

The United States is not the only country that has developed such a warning system. Of all the countries in the world, Japan has experienced the highest number of destructive tsunamis. In 1952, Japan created its own Tsunami Warning Service (TWS), run by the Japan Meteorological Society. Today the TWS is the most efficient warning system in the world. Thousands of earthquake sensors and eighty water-level gauges are located around the country. Japanese scientists have developed a computer program that predicts the height, speed, and arrival time of

A Tsunami Story from Old Japan

A wealthy old farmer named Hamaguchi Gohei lived on a hill overlooking a bayside village of about four hundred inhabitants near Osaka. Hamaguchi was the village *choja*, a trusted and respected leader. One evening, Hamaguchi was at home with his ten-year-old grandson, Tada. The ground began to tremble, and Hamaguchi recognized the familiar sensation of a mild earthquake. As the shaking stopped, Hamaguchi gazed out to sea and gasped. He knew something was terribly wrong because the water was moving against the wind; it was retreating from the land.

Recalling stories told by his own grandfather, Hamaguchi knew he must warn the villagers immediately. He told Tada to light a pine torch. Then he hurried to his fields where the harvested rice stalks lay in piles, ready for market. As fast as his old legs would carry him, Hamaguchi rushed from pile to pile and set the stalks on fire. Tada begged his grandfather to stop. Why was he burning up the family's entire source of income? But Hamaguchi didn't stop to explain. He knew there was no time to waste.

Smoke billowed into the twilight sky. In the village, the priest rang the temple bell to summon the people. Several young men ran up the hill and reached the rice fields, but Hamaguchi refused to let them put out the fire. Sobbing, Tada told the men that his grandfather must have gone mad because he had set the fire himself.

As soon as all the villagers reached the top of the hill, Hamaguchi pointed to the sea and shouted, "Say now if I be mad!"* In the dim light, the villagers saw the sea returning to shore, "towering like a cliff, and coursing more swiftly than the kite flies."*

They screamed, "Tsunami!"—but their voices were swallowed by the thundering roar of the giant wave. Suddenly, a cloud of spray blocked their view of their homes. Then they watched the sea engulf their village. Five times, the giant waves attacked the shore. When the water finally receded, the land where the village had been was bare. All that could be seen of the people's homes were two straw roofs tossing in the wild ocean.

Then Hamaguchi said, "That was why I set fire to the rice."* Tada ran to hug his grandfather, and the villagers bowed with gratitude.

When at last the people were able to rebuild their homes, they also built a shrine in honor of their *choja*, who had sacrificed his wealth to save their lives.

*The quotations are from "The Living God," the original version of this story by Lafcadio Hearn, a schoolteacher who lived in Japan. The story is said to be based on a real event that happened during the 1854 tsunami. Often retold, the story is sometimes called "Fire in the Haystalks."

a tsunami triggered by any Pacific-region earthquake. Within three minutes, Japanese scientists can broadcast an alert by siren and on TV and radio.

These warning systems have certainly saved lives all over the Pacific. But they rely on expensive instruments and around-the-clock monitoring by skilled scientists. Because of the cost, the other oceans of the world have no warning system in place. Officials thought they couldn't justify the cost because tsunamis outside the Pacific are so rare. But after the horrific experience of the 2004 tsunami in the Indian Ocean, world leaders have changed their minds. Both scientists and authorities are now committed to creating a warning system in the Indian Ocean and elsewhere.

GETTING OUT OF HARM'S WAY

Tsunami warnings are based on careful analysis. But they will only save lives if people understand the danger. Only six years after the deadly April Fools' Day disaster, the PTWC issued a warning about an approaching tsunami. After hearing the warning, some people actually hurried *toward*—rather than away from—the beaches in Hawaii! Honolulu police officers risked their lives rounding up these sightseers.

Even along shores where deadly tsunamis have previously struck, people may underestimate the threat. During the 1960 tsunami in Hilo, onlookers were killed when they hurried to the seashore to watch the waves.

Police have had to stop surfers from running into the water after a tsunami warning has been broadcast. Apparently these daredevils thought a tsunami would provide "the ride of a lifetime." In reality, surfing a tsunami would probably be the last ride of a surfer's life.

Vacationers visiting tsunami-prone coasts often know nothing about this threat from the sea. In 1994, some tourists were totally baffled after hearing a tsunami alert in Hawaii. Although they spoke English, they misunderstood the broadcast and wondered why everyone was getting excited about a "salami warning!" Of course, nobody wants to frighten vacationers, but visitors as well as coastal residents need to be educated about tsunamis.

How Are People along Threatened Coasts Warned of a Coming Tsunami?

Some communities have thought up clever solutions, such as warnings delivered by automatic dial-up to residents' phones. Along beaches, public address systems have

been installed to broadcast warnings. Evacuation routes are frequently marked on road signs. Japan has constructed sea walls and river flood-gates on many of its tsunami-prone coastlines. And in Japanese schools located near coastlines, students practice tsunami drills, similar to fire drills. In Hawaii, public telephone books contain maps showing tsunami danger zones and the locations of shelters. In Oregon, laws prevent the building of fire and police stations, as well as hospitals, in zones likely to be flooded by tsunamis. In northern Chile, power poles are painted red in areas that might be flooded during a tsunami.

Can People Build Structures That Can Withstand the Force of a Tsunami?

Yes, but the most powerful tsunamis may overwhelm even the best-designed structures. During past disasters, structures made of reinforced concrete have proven to be most effective in withstanding both tsunami waves and the earthquakes. Hotels with open ground floors have also withstood the waves by allowing water to rush through the lowest level while the upper stories remain intact.

Research into tsunami-resistant structures continues. Scientists in Japan are working on "smart" seawalls for the future. One model will flutter to reduce the force of the wave. Another will have a core that senses the size of a wave and rises in response.

Because of the disastrous 2004 tsunami in the Indian Ocean, scientists are now working harder than ever to refine tsunami warning systems. Both scientists and government officials are developing warning systems to protect people outside the Pacific basin. Countries are exchanging ideas about how to alert people who live on remote shores.

But the biggest obstacle to keeping people safe may be people themselves. After a few months, news reports about a deadly tsunami become "old news." People have short memories, and even coastal residents forget how sudden and devastating a tsunami can be. Newcomers move to coastal communities every year, and tourists arrive to enjoy sun and surf. That's why tsunami education—as well as scientific research—is an ongoing task.

Can you surf a tsunami?

No. It's true that expert surfers can ride enormous ocean waves, but tsunami waves aren't like the typical wind waves that roll toward land. Tsunami waves do not form a curl that a surfer can ride. Instead, a tsunami wave is more like a flood or the rushing whitewater of a wild river. In such a surge of water, a surfer cannot control the ride. Nobody knows how many misguided surfers have been killed when they grabbed their boards and plunged into the ocean to catch a ride on a tsunami.

In 1974, a world champion surfer named Filipe Pomar happened to be surfing off Peru when a tsunami arrived. Pomar wasn't looking for "the ride of a lifetime." A combination of luck, strength, and skill saved his life.

Only one other report exists of a person who surfed a tsunami and lived to tell about it. During Hawaii's 1868 tsunami, a couple fled from their home in Ninole, just a few miles south of Laupahoehoe. But Holoua, the husband, foolishly decided to run back home to retrieve some money. While he was inside, a wave engulfed his house and swept it out to sea. Holoua managed to rip a board off the house. Using this as a surfboard, he jumped aboard and struck out for shore. People standing on a nearby hill were amazed to see this powerful man riding a fifty-foot wall of water to safety!

MEGA-TSUNAMIS

As devastating as tsunamis have been during recorded history, scientists have found evidence of far worse events that happened during prehistoric times. These tsunamis produced waves higher than the skyline of some of today's major cities. They are called "mega-tsunamis."

What causes a mega-tsunami? Scientists believe that massive landslides usually trigger them. In most cases, these landslides were produced when a whole flank of a volcano near an ocean broke off and fell into the water.

In Hawaii, scientists believe they have found evidence of a mega-tsunami that occurred about 110,000 years ago. The evidence comes from fossil remains of ocean animals found on the Big Island. These fossils were discovered on high slopes—land that never has been covered by the sea. How could ocean animals have died there? One theory claims that they were deposited by a mega-tsunami with waves taller than New York's Empire State Building! The origin of this mega-tsunami was probably a landslide caused by the collapse of a flank of the huge volcano, Mauna Loa.

EXTRATERRESTRIAL TSUNAMIS?

A huge landslide from an entire flank of a volcano is an unusual event. But a mega-tsunami may sometimes be caused by something even more unusual: a large asteroid from space plummeting into an ocean on Earth.

Scientists have found evidence suggesting two massive asteroids hit Earth more than three billion years ago. The extent of the damage is hard to imagine—it's more like a science-fiction

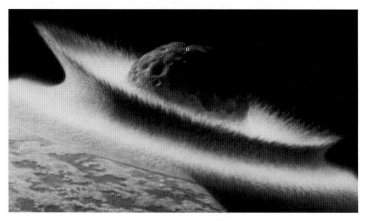

movie than an actual event! These asteroids may have been twenty miles in diameter, which is about as long as Martha's Vineyard, an island off the coast of Massachusetts. When such large asteroids collided with Earth, they would have produced mega-tsunamis that swept around our planet several times. Waves would have covered all landmasses except the tallest

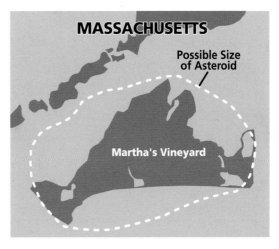

mountains, and most living creatures would have been killed.

Some scientists believe that a smaller asteroid, about six miles wide, may have caused the extinction of the dinosaurs sixty-five million years ago. It probably struck near Mexico's Yucatan Peninsula and produced a mega-tsunami that extinguished the lives of millions of animals.

Scientists at the Los Alamos National Laboratory in New Mexico have calculated the damage that an asteroid three miles wide would do if it slammed into the middle of the Atlantic Ocean. According to their findings, the collision would produce a tsunami that would wash inland as far as the Appalachian Mountains. Water would bury the eastern seaboard, including Boston, New York City, and Washington, D.C.!

Could a massive asteroid be headed our way? Researchers at the University of California Santa Cruz are tracking one (called "Asteroid 1950 DA") that measures half a mile wide. This asteroid is expected to swing close to Earth in about eight hundred years, but scientists do not think that a collision is likely. According to computer simulations, if this asteroid were to collide with our planet, it would cause a mega-tsunami with waves taller than the Eiffel Tower.

But the good news is that asteroids are one natural disaster that scientists can predict with accuracy. By the time an asteroid would approach Earth, scientists and officials would surely have a plan ready to protect people.

When Will the Next Mega-Tsunami Occur?

Nobody knows. Fortunately, mega-tsunamis are very rare. An event this large probably happens only once in about one hundred thousand years.

According to a recent study, volcanic landslides happen more often during Earth's warmer periods, when the climate is rainier and sea levels are higher. All the excess rainwater seeping into porous volcanic material eventually enlarges natural cracks and causes a flank to break loose.

Kilauea Volcano, Hawaii

This study is disturbing because Earth is now in one of its warm periods, with rising temperatures and higher sea levels. Does this mean that you should add the threat of a mega-tsunami to your list of greatest fears? Probably not. These events are predicted to happen over extremely long time periods—called geological ages—rather than human lifetimes. Scientists calculate that there's only a fifty percent chance that a mega-tsunami might occur anytime in the next ten thousand years.

How can you help?

Immediately after a tsunami strikes, survivors need food, water, medicine, clothing, and blankets. When the initial crisis is over, they need help rebuilding their homes, businesses, and communities. Organizations like the Red Cross, CARE, Habitat for Humanity, and UNICEF often launch fundraising campaigns for the victims of tsunamis. These organizations can be contacted through their Web sites.

Working through schools and churches, children can help by collecting donations. (Remember: For safety's sake, young people should request adult guidance before going door to door or approaching strangers.) In addition to relief efforts, children can help with tsunami education. If you visit or live near a coastline, notice the evacuation routes. Ask about how warnings will be broadcast. Memorize the natural warning signals. Share your knowledge with your family and friends. Like Tilly Smith from England, anyone can be a helper when disaster strikes.

Expert Advice

If you feel an earthquake, if you see shore water retreating, or if you hear a loud roar from the ocean, what should you do?

Be prepared. If you live in or visit an area at risk of tsunamis—such as Hawaii, Cascadia, and Alaska—educate yourself. Learn how authorities send out warnings. Find out: Will a siren go off? Will it have a distinctive tone?

Memorize the natural warning signals, too. According to Eddie Bernard, director of Seattle's Pacific Marine Environmental Laboratory, "If you feel an earthquake, if you see the water retreating, or if you hear a loud roar from the ocean, . . . head inland fast." Even if you can't get to higher ground, every step away from the ocean will take you one step farther from danger. And don't wait for the official notice to evacuate.

Bernard advises residents of threatened areas to fill a backpack with essentials for a few days. Once you recognize a natural tsunami-warning signal, "grab that backpack on your way out of your house," he says.

Is it safer to evacuate by foot or by car? Surprisingly, most experts recommend moving by foot. Along many coasts, only one road leads inland, and people trying to leave in their vehicles would quickly jam it. A car stalled in traffic can become a deathtrap, so experts urge people to carry only essentials and rely on their legs to get out of danger.

EARTH'S OCEANS: BENEFITS AND DANGERS

People have always enjoyed a beneficial relationship with the world's oceans. These refreshing, aquamarine waters provide us with food and transport, as well as recreation and beauty. But the ocean can turn deadly with little warning. Even under sunny skies, as innocent children joke and play along the shore, the ocean may suddenly give birth to the catastrophe we call a "tsunami."

After giant waves engulfed a Hawaiian schoolyard in 1946, people read with horror the details of the disaster. The tsunami in the schoolyard taught the world a deadly lesson and inspired American scientists in the Pacific Basin to create a warning system to protect human lives. After an even more devastating tsunami in the Indian Ocean in 2004, scientists around the world are now working to extend this warning system to people who live near all the world's oceans.

FOR FURTHER INFORMATION

BOOKS

Dudley, Walter C. and Min Lee. *Tsunami!* Second edition. Honolulu: University of Hawaii Press, 1998. Contains detailed accounts of Hawaiian tsunamis, including eyewitness accounts from the 1946 and 1960 disasters. Chapters cover the science of tsunamis, major tsunamis throughout history, and how the Pacific Tsunami Warning System works.

Knight, Gary, James Nachtwey, and Simon Winchester. *Tsunami: A Document of Devastation.* Edited by Giorgio Baravalle. Millbrook, New York: De.MO, 2005. Loose-leaf photo collection measures 38" by 25" when open. Poster-sized photos seem to transport the viewer to Indonesia and Sri Lanka to witness the destruction caused by the 2004 Indian Ocean tsunami.

Krauss, Erich. *Wave of Destruction: The Stories of Four Families and History's Deadliest Tsunami.* Emmaus, PA: Rodale, 2006. A powerful nonfiction account of the lives and struggles of four families in Nam Khem, a small village on the coast of Thailand, before, during, and after a tsunami destroys their village. Amazing survival stories.

Stewart, Gail B. *Catastrophe in Southern Asia: The Tsunami of 2004.* Detroit: Lucent Books, 2005. A straightforward account for young adult readers. Focuses on the issues facing survivors and officials in the aftermath of the disaster, such as the death toll, grief, hygiene, and rebuilding communities.

Tibballs, Geoff. *Tsunami: The World's Most Terrifying Natural Disaster.* London: Carlton Books, 2005. Eyewitness accounts and statistics of deaths, injuries, and damage from the areas hardest hit by the 2004 Indian Ocean tsunami. Includes photos of the waves, the destruction, and the coastal communities (before and after).

WEB SITES

http://www.ess.washington.edu/tsunami/index.html
Hosted by the University of Washington's Department of Earth and Space Sciences. Features up-to-date messages from tsunami warning centers and links to Web sites about recent tsunamis and technical info.

http://www.enchantedlearning.com/subjects/tsunami/
Enchanted Learning's Web site features a kid-friendly overview of the causes and behavior of tsunamis. Includes a glossary, a list of major tsunamis in history, and an activities page. Downloadable maps, diagrams, a coloring sheet, and a short, printable book.

http://www.tsunami.org/
The Pacific Tsunami Museum site includes photos of tsunami damage in Hawaii, accounts written by survivors, an explanation of the causes of tsunamis, and a talking virtual robot that answers questions.

http://www.pbs.org/wgbh/nova/tsunami/
Visitors to the PBS site may download a transcript of the *Nova* program "Wave That Shook the World." Also included: an article about the science of tsunamis, a description of major tsunamis in history, and a detailed "Ask the Expert" Q&A section.

http://www.usc.edu/dept/tsunamis/2005/index.php
The Web site for the University of Southern California's Tsunami Research Center. Includes news articles about tsunamis and reports about current research, as well as animations of simulated tsunamis and videos of actual tsunamis striking shores.

VIDEOS

"Tsunami: Wave of Disaster." Discovery Channel, 2005. TV documentary featuring footage of the 2004 Indian Ocean tsunami and interviews with survivors.

"Wave That Shook the World." *Nova.* PBS, 2005. TV documentary featuring footage of the 2004 Indian Ocean tsunami and interviews with survivors, journalists, and scientists. Includes information about the formation of tsunamis and scientific progress in understanding these disasters.

BIBLIOGRAPHY

BOOKS

April Fool's…The Laupahoehoe Tragedy of 1946; an Oral History. Honolulu: Obun Hawaii, Inc. for the Laupahoehoe School, 1997.

Atwater, Brian F., Joanne Bourgeois, Marco Cisternas, Walter C. Dudley, James W. Hendley II, and Peter H. Stauffer. *Surviving a Tsunami—Lessons from Chile, Hawaii, and Japan.* U.S. Geological Survey Circular; 1187. Reston, VA: U.S. Dept. of the Interior and U.S. Geological Survey, 1999.

Dudley, Walter C. *Tsunamis in Hawaii.* Hilo, Hawaii: Pacific Tsunami Museum, 1999.

Dudley, Walter C. and Scott C.S. Stone. *The Tsunami of 1946 and 1960 and the Devastation of Hilo Town.* Virginia Beach: Donning Company, 2000.

Dudley, Walter C. and Min Lee. *Tsunami!* Second edition. Honolulu: University of Hawaii Press, 1998.

Waiakea High School Booklet 1998–99. Hilo: Waiakea High School Tsunami Network, 1999.

WEB SITES

April Fools' Day Tsunami
Davidson, Sarah. "Mystery of Deadly 1946 Tsunami Deepens." *LiveScience*, December 6, 2004. http://www.livescience.com/forcesofnature/041206_ tsunami_new.html

Deadly History
Adler, Jerry and Mary Carmichael. "The Tsunami Threat." *Newsweek*, January 10, 2005. http://www.msnbc.msn.com/id/6777713/site/newsweek/

"Asia's Tsunami." *Time.* http://www.time.com/time/ photoessays/tsunami

"The Deadliest Tsunami in History?" *National Geographic News*, January 7, 2005. http://news.nationalgeographic.com/ news/2004/12/1227_041226_tsunami.html

Dengler, Lori. "Ask the Expert Responses." PBS Online. http://www.pbs.org/wgbh/nova/tsunami/ask.html

Disaster in Asia; Interactive Map. http://www.cbc.ca.news/back-ground/asia_earthquake/cbcairgrid/cbcnews?dia.html

"Hell, High Water, and Heartache." *CBC News*, April 21, 2005. http://www.cbc.ca/news/background/asia_earthquake/

McGhee, Geoff, Judith Schlieper, Eric Owles, and Lisa Laboni. "Asia's Deadly Waves." *New York Times*, December 27, 2004. http://www.nytimes.com/packages/html/ international/ 20041227_QUAKE_FEATURE

National Oceanic and Atmospheric Administration, National Weather Service. "About Tsunamis." West Coast & Alaska Tsunami Warning Center. http://wcatwc.arh.noaa.gov/sub-page1.htm

"Once and Future Tsunamis." PBS Online. http://www.pbs.org/wgbh/nova/tsunami/once.html

Pendrick, Daniel. "A Deadly Force." PBS Online. http://www.pbs.org/ wnet/savageearth/tsunami/

Schmid, Randolphe E. "Sunday's Tidal Wave Rivals Past Tsunamis." *The Daily Herald*, December 30, 2004. http://www.harktheherald.com/content/view/109383/

"Thailand's Tsunami Anniversary." *CBS News*, December 24, 2005. http://www.cbsnews.com/ stories/2005/12/24/world/ main1165157.shtml?CMP=OTC-RSSFeed&source=RSS &attr= HOME_1165157

Tyson, Peter. "Wave of the Future." PBS Online. www.pbs.org/wgbh/nova/ tsunami/wave.html

Gift from the Sea
Biswas, Soutik. "Tsunami Throws Up India Relics." *BBC News*, February 11, 2005. http://news.bbc.co.uk/ 1/hi/world/ south_asia/4257181.stm

Philp, Catherine. "Mystery of the Smiling Buddha and Ancient Carvings That Arrived as a Gift from the Tsunami." *The Times Online*, May 31, 2005. http://travel.times online.co.uk

"Tsunami Brings Ancient Ruins to Light." *Taipei Times*, February 19, 2005. http://www.taipeitimes.com/ News/world/archives/2005/02/19/2003223679

Mega-Tsunami
Britt, Robert Roy. "The Megatsunami: Possible Modern Threat." *LiveScience*, December 14, 2004. http://www.livescience.com/ forcesofnature/041214_tsunami_ mega.html

"Prehistoric Asteroid 'Killed Everything.'" *National Geographic News*, August 23, 2002. http://news.nationalgeographic.com/news/2002/08/0823_020823_asteroid.html

Sound the Warning!

Dahanayake, Kapila. "Tsunami Early Warning System—How It Works." *Daily News* (Sri Lanka), March 22, 2005. http://dailynews.lk

Hall, Kenji. "Researchers Study Tallest Man-Made Tsunami." *Boston Globe*, June 30, 2005. http://www.boston.com/news/science/articles/2005/06/30/researchers_study_tallest_man_made_tsunami/

Lovgren, Stefan. "Tsunamis More Likely to Hit U.S. Than Asia." *National Geographic News*, January 3, 2005. http://news.nationalgeographic.com/news/2005/01/0103_050103_US_tsunami.html

Miyazaki, Jamie. "How Japan Handles Tsunami Threat." *BBC News*, May 1, 2005. http://news.bbc.co.uk/2/hi/asia-pacific/4149009.stm

Simkin, Mark. "Japan Likely to Take Lead in Tsunami Warning System." *ABC Online*, January 6, 2005. http://www.abc.net.au/pm/content/2005/s1277760.htm

Wiseman, Paul. "Politics Enters Plan for Tsunami Warning System." *USA Today*, March 2, 2005. http://www.usatoday.com/news/world/2005-03-02-tsunami-warning-system_x.htm

Student Gets A+ for Tsunami Lesson

Associated Press. "Schoolgirl Saves Nearly 100 Lives." *Fox News*, January 2, 2005. http://www.foxnews.com/story/0,2933,143092,00.html

Owen, James. "Tsunami Family Saved by Schoolgirl's Geography Lesson." *National Geographic News*, January 18, 2005. http://news.nationalgeographic.com/news/2005/01/0118_050118_tsunami_geography_lesson.html

Wiseman, Paul. "Politics Enters Plan for Tsunami Warning System." *USA Today*, March 2, 2005. http://www.usatoday.com/news/world/2005-03-02-tsunamiwarning-system_x.htm

Tsunami Warning in Old Japan

Hearn, Lafcadio. "Inamura No Hi—The Living God." http://www.inamuranohi.jp/english.html

Japan International Cooperation Agency. "An Old Folklore Has Found a Place in the Heart of Both Japanese and Cambodian Children." http://www.jica.go.jp/english/resources/publications/network/200503/20050307.html

Koizuma, Junichiro. "Address by Junichiro Koizumi, Prime Minister of Japan, at the United Nations World Conference on Disaster Reduction." Kobe, Japan, January 18, 2005. http://www.kantei.go.jp/foreign/koizumispeech/2005/01/18address_e.html

Mahendra, Sunanda. "Tsunami and the Creative Awareness." *Daily News* (Sri Lanka), January 19, 2005. http://www.dailynews.lk/2005/01/19/artscop02.html

INTERVIEWS

Kawaihona Laeha Poy of Laupahoehoe, Hawaii. Telephone interview by Gail Karwoski. February 11, 2005.

Transcripts from the Pacific Tsunami Museum, Hilo, Hawaii, of the following interviews:

Frank DeCaires
Mr. and Mrs. Clarence Ferdun; report and oral interview conducted July 22, 1998
Bunji Fujimoto; interview conducted March 3, 1999
Bill Choy Hee
Mona Malani
Marsue McGinnis McShane
Herbert Nishimoto
Ronald Yamaoka

DOCUMENTARIES AND TELEVISION BROADCASTS

America's Tsunami: Are We Next? DVD. Discovery Channel. http://dsc.discovery.com/tvlistings/episode.jsp?episode=1&cpi=30464&gid=0&channel=DSC

"Asian Tsunami: One Year Later." *Paula Zahn Now*. CNN. December 26, 2005. http://transcripts.cnn.com/TRANSCRIPTS/0512/26/pzn.01.html

Tsunami 2004: Waves of Death DVD. History Channel.

Tsunami: Killer Wave. The Wrath of God series. DVD. History Channel.

Tsunami: Wave of Disaster. DVD. Discovery Channel. http://dsc.discovery.com/tvlistings/episode.jsp?episode=0&cpi=25251&gid=0&channel=DSC

"Wave That Shook the World." *Nova*. PBS. March 29, 2005. http://www.pbs.org/wgbh/nova/transcripts/3208_tsunami.htm